Affiliate Marketing

Each Advice And Strategy Is Presented Succinctly, With Actionable Steps To Help You Effectively Implement The Strategies

(How To Generate Revenue As An Affiliate Marketer)

Luther Dickerson

TABLE OF CONTENT

Introduction 1

How To Sell Properly 8

Choosing The Appropriate Affiliate Program 17

Putting Everything Together 19

Conclusion 22

Your Life Freedom 25

Business Models For Affiliate Marketing 32

Conclusion 40

What You Need To Know Concerning Affiliate Commission Payment Schedules 42

How To Locate Items That Will Sell In Your Drop Shipping Store 58

Other Strategies 93

Add Affiliate Links To Your Free Reports 95

Maintaining Affiliates' Interest And Participation 108

What Is The Level Of Competition In Affiliate Marketing? 112

Optimizing Your Ads 127

Some Requirements For Every Marketer 136

Introduction

Numerous affiliate marketers earn six-figure incomes and more. You can also accomplish this. There is no need for you to promote your products and services if you are utilizing subsidiary marketing. It is also unnecessary to have a well-known brand.

If you have significant doubts about making a fortune through affiliate marketing, you should consider the following. There is abundant evidence that many partners are generating a large deal of revenue from their missions.

In subsidiary marketing, you promote the products or services of others for a commission. You can advance physical items, such as those found on

Amazon.com, or digital products from member organizations such as Clickbank.com. Alternatively, you may promote both physical and digital products if you so choose.

In general, the commissions you will earn from advancing physical items will be modest. They typically range between 3% and 8%. Generally speaking, the commissions for computerized products will be substantially higher. You can find computerized products to sell that pay between 50 and 100 percent commissions. However, it is simpler to sell physical products.

New item shipments are an effective method for generating predictable subsidiary commissions. These are exceptionally popular in the online moneymaking niche. Each day, new items are shipped in this niche, and you can become their subsidiary and earn commissions by promoting them.

By no means are item dispatches the only method for members to earn commissions. You have probably heard the phrase "the money is in the rundown." This refers to having an email list of supporters who are interested in your chosen specialty.

As a subsidiary, you can send them automated and broadcast messages promoting new and existing products and services. When you decide to create a product in your area of expertise, you can promote it directly to your email subscribers.

Email marketing is one of the best methods to generate revenue with member marketing, and we strongly recommend that you create an email list. Try not to believe that email marketing is extinct because it is not. It will be a compelling method of promotion for an indefinite period of time.

A further option is to conduct item surveys. Creating video surveys and uploading them to YouTube can be highly engaging. It is much simpler to rank a survey video highly on YouTube than it is to position a blog post highly using web search tools. Frequently, recordings also rank on the first page of web crawlers.

Anyone can become a member advertiser with minimal effort. We strongly recommend that you purchase your domain name and web hosting. This is preferable to using a free website or blog service such as Weebly or WordPress.

Today's Internet-savvy individuals are aware of whether or not a blog is gratis. You are endeavoring to convince your guests to purchase the ancillary products you are promoting. Why should they put stock in you in the event that you can't be tried to purchase your domain name and hosting?

Here are the primary benefits of being an advertiser member:

You are not required to produce your items.

There are numerous associate proposals for you to promote.

You are not required to manage any client service issues, such as discounts.

You do not need to carry or transport any inventory.

You can be an effective affiliate marketer at home.

The cost of travel is extremely minimal.

You can advance products in a few specialized categories.

These are the primary reasons why there are so many affiliate marketplaces attempting to earn commissions by promoting others' products and services. A small proportion of these individuals are successful for various reasons.

There is no requirement for insight to succeed in affiliate marketing. If you are a proficient internet marketer, you can propose affiliate programs to increase your earnings. Once you have established your partner promotion efforts, they can become a source of recurring, automated revenue.

We believe that in order to be an effective member advertiser, you must have a thorough understanding of the most extensively used terminology in the industry. In this comprehensive report, we will provide you with a subsidiary marketing A-Z glossary with definitions of each term.

How To Sell Properly

The six elements that must be present in your proposals to attract buyers:

People mistake proposals for the goods or services they are attempting to sell. Wrong! In reality, an offer is much more than the product or service you intend to deliver. The offer is the total value you provide in exchange for payment.

A proposal is based on:

Cost/Pricing

Attractive Risk Reversal (Money Back Guarantee) Discounts (Accurate Discounting)

Bonuses. How many? Which Benefits?

Project requires

Creating anticipation for:

Pricing

The price you set for your services must be reasonable for your customers and profitable for your company. You are free to set any price for your services. Pricing is a minor component of your offering. From past experience, clients who are price-conscious are the worst customers.

Cost-plus pricing?

Value-based pricing is a pricing strategy based on the perceived value of a product or service to the consumer. Value pricing is customer-focused pricing, which means that companies base their prices on the perceived value of a product to the consumer.

Value-based pricing differs from "cost-plus" pricing, which includes production expenses in the price calculation. Companies that offer distinctive or highly valuable characteristics or services are better positioned to benefit from the value pricing model than those that primarily sell commodities.

Attention-grabbing Risk Reversal

Risk reversal gives the consumer a sense of safety. It is the response to the question "What will occur if I (common_objective)?" I offer a money-back guarantee of 100 percent if I fail to deliver.

Ideas for Risk Reversal.

Cancel anytime

Unlimited modifications

In excess of a money-back guarantee

Emotional Assurance (No hassles, rapid customer service)

No obligations

Payment terms (50 percent now, 50 percent upon delivery)

Cash -guarantee(you can provide a thirty-day window)

Discounts

Offer discounts on special dates or to customers referred by their peers or other customers.

Reduce Costs Appropriately

The discount should be straightforward. In the example given below, there is a $20 discount.

Main price: $50

Investment: $30 (discounted rate)

You can also use contrast principle

When addressing price objections, you can use the contrast principle to make the cost of your offer appear lower. The purpose of this comparison is to make your price appear less costly.

See the contrast principle illustration below:

The initial price establishes the tone. It serves as an anchor. It remains in the client's consciousness, making $500 appear to be less than it is.

The customer may think, "Wow, $1000 for a sales funnel? "I'll only have to pay $500 for it."

Now, here are a few suggestions for offering incentives.

Instead of giving them away in the proposition, use them as a negotiating tool.

See the example given below.

Client: "You know, Henry, $1000 is still a bit beyond my budget."

Me: "I completely comprehend your point of view. You seek the finest value-based offer for your business. So, let me explain what I can do for you. Would you sign the contract if I included a free domain and one year of hosting (a $250 value) for no additional cost?

This is the proper response to objections. You can use bonuses to achieve objectives and persuade customers to make purchases.

Adding incentives to your offers increases their perceived value to customers.

Project requires

Each endeavor or service has its own challenges to overcome. During the "Pitching your offer" phase, you will determine which issue you will need to address.

As a result, don't worry excessively about this, as you can simply speak to your clients and exchange emails to determine their goals.

Creating anticipation

Document the extent of the service.

What will you be delivering?

How do you plan to deliver it?

Are the services divided into multiple phases?

Who will give final approval?

What occurs if consumers request additional revisions following approval?

business tools

Selling a variety of products - including digital, services, and physical - is significantly more effective because it combines the enormous sales that can be generated by cultivating a loyal audience with the VOLUME that results from moving large quantities of physical products.

Scaleo is among the top affiliate marketing software on the market. It permits you to monitor your paid and organic affiliate marketing activities down to the level of conversion. As an affiliate marketer, it is essential to comprehend which aspects of your campaign generate revenue. Consequently, you will need the proper ad monitoring tool to detect this data.

Scaleo's cutting-edge tracker technology enables centralized management of all paid campaigns.

Planner for Google AdWords keywords:

Beginners in affiliate marketing should also have access to the Google Keyword Planner. It's a free Google tool that allows you to view keyword-related data at a high level. It is entirely free to use, and it is unquestionably the most precise instrument available.

It enables you to scrutinize the anticipated monthly volume generated by a particular keyword, its cost, and the level of competition, among other things. This is an excellent strategy for conducting keyword research if you do not wish to pay for a service.

Choosing The Appropriate Affiliate Program

Commission Junction Market is a network that provides advertisers and publishers with access to relevant information, results analysis, and product management. It promises publishers generous compensation. How it works for advertisers and publishers is outlined below.

Advertisers utilize CJ Market's reporting tools to create call-to-action buttons, define program terms, publish application evaluations, and analyze program performance. In addition, they offer CJU Online, an online resource for learning strategies, connecting with publishers, and discovering the most recent industry news.

Publishers: You can submit an application to join programs and have access to the entire link directory. Then, you can begin placing offers on your website, in e-mail campaigns, and in search engine listings.

There are additional methods to discover affiliate programs that operate independently of affiliate networks. Not included in the directories. Obtaining information about them can be somewhat more problematic. If you learn of a sale, you can always email the merchant directly to inquire about specifics.

Occasionally, you may encounter a program labeled "Invite Only." These sites typically restrict access by admitting only people who have purchased their product or by evaluating and approving individuals on an individual basis.

Putting Everything Together

You are now completely knowledgeable about social media marketing. We've gotten as specific as delineating your strategy and content calendar. Now, we will take the final step of 'fitting it all together.' In other words, we will take all of these steps and construct a plan that you can implement immediately.

It is crucial that you read this chapter in its entirety. It's simple to feel like you have everything figured out, but you need to know how to put the tools you've created into action.

First, plan your content in minute detail.

Planning your content in minute detail is essential to ensuring that you understand precisely what you must do to produce excellent content. Examine what others have done that has been successful as a starting point. You may become overwhelmed if you spend too much time on this, but you should spend enough time to get a decent idea of what to do. Plan how your content will appear and what it will say as you search. Keep note of each and every detail.

Step 2: Reserve Time, Create, and Market!

Next, schedule time to create the content that you intend to publish. If you have planned ahead, you should have ample time to complete this task with excellence. Ensure that you are pleased with the content you create, as it will represent your brand. You want to create content that accurately represents your brand. Take your time and incorporate chapter 3's exposure measures. When you're set, publish your content and promote it!

Step Three: Evaluate Your Strategy

Finally, it is essential to evaluate your strategy. Every 3 to 4 weeks, evaluate the content you've been producing to determine if you're meeting your objectives. If not, analyze your content to determine where you are not achieving the desired results and what you can do to enhance them. Make only minor adjustments to your strategy at any given time so you can determine what is working and what is not. Changes that occur too frequently and in excess can cause your content to become disorganized and perplexing, causing you to lose results.

Conclusion

Affiliate marketing is not for people who give up easily or jump from one trend to the next without giving each one a reasonable chance. It takes time to amass resources, such as blog traffic and email lists, because it requires a great deal of effort. There are no fast fixes unless you have the financial means to pay for content creation, the purchase of already popular websites, or the acquisition of a large number of email addresses and social media followers. When you enter the perilous field of affiliate marketing, keep these mistakes in mind. Make sure you're not doing any of these things, and if you begin to see financial success, don't let up on your efforts. These errors can be committed by anyone! Making money is assured if you exert effort, persist, and avoid making these mistakes.

This concludes the comprehensive and exhaustive guide to establishing a profitable affiliate marketing business. Whether you want to keep things simple or reach for the stars is up to you, but if you take away anything from this book, let it be this: in addition to digital eBooks and courses, consider selling authentic products with widespread appeal and high prices. Finding a digital product with an affiliate link, creating a sales page for it, embedding the affiliate link on the page, and driving traffic to the page through your own website and other marketing channels constitutes traditional affiliate product marketing. Rather than waiting until the item stops selling and starting over, I suggest you modify this strategy considerably to generate more revenue and develop a more sustainable, long-term business strategy. Here is the revised strategy:

Establishing a website where your followers can interact with you and learn more about you is the first step in establishing a loyal following for your online work. Create content that is truly unique and driven by your company's core values and guiding principles; "launch" a handful of high-ticket affiliate goods and services from your website using email blasts and teasers to generate buzz; identify and promote your most profitable offerings, and drive more traffic to your website through paid advertising. You can now earn money while sleeping, and the more you experiment, the more effective your sales strategy will be.

Your Life Freedom

You are likely interested in affiliate marketing because of the leisure it appears to offer.

It sounds appealing to be able to set up systems that generate income while you sleep, work, or spend time with your family.

I get it.

Working a 9-to-5 job, whether in a factory or an office, is arduous. Doing something you don't want to do for so long is mentally depleting.

There is no assurance that you will attain the freedom of your life and leisure, or that you will get there any time soon.

It depends on how you construct your systems and how you compensate employees to replace you.

Yes, replace you.

My primary objective in my business is to always replace myself at a higher level.

A few months ago, I struggled to produce sufficient content for my websites.

As previously stated, I would write at most one or two articles per week during pauses and lunch at my full-time job. It was a terrible sensation to have so many ideas for business-enhancing articles but no time to execute them.

I felt genuinely stuck. I lacked the time to complete higher-level tasks, such as composing this book and strategizing for my business, because I was preoccupied with the fundamental task of content creation.

Then I chose to employ a writer. I supplanted myself as the business's writer. This is the first position in which I have supplanted myself. I consider myself an SEO and content expert and have a full-time job proving this. I employed a writer and instructed her in blogging and SEO; consequently, I no longer produce as many articles.

Why did I supplant myself in the area where I excel?

Life liberty.

My ultimate objective is to have a business that largely operates itself, where I am the owner and have the freedom to pursue creative activities and spend a great deal more time with my family without financial constraints.

As a writer, if I supplanted everything but myself, I would still have to work. A job I own, but a job nonetheless. Exchanging leisure for cash.

Once I had replaced myself as the writer, I was receiving 4-5 articles per week AND my writer enjoys creating graphics, so I did not have to spend time creating graphics for the blog post AND she was creating favorites for our Pinterest account. More productivity and expansion.

This story's purpose is not to boast that I have people working for me to save time. The purpose is also not to demonstrate my lack of a full-fledged business where I'm currently relaxing on a beach at a resort while others make money for me.

The objective is that affiliate marketing is a process for achieving life freedom.

Know that it's a process, it takes time, but the final result is so rewarding, whether you're hiring people with money you earn from your business or purchasing software to help automate your processes while you still run things yourself.

Consider your ultimate objective right now, whether it is financial and time independence or something else wholly. Put it down on paper. Place it where it can be seen. This is what will keep you going during the difficult times when you just want to give up.

Your liberation awaits you. The destination is out there. You need only invest time and effort to acquire it. Two to three years of arduous effort are preferable to twenty to forty years of effort spent making someone else's aspirations come true.

Now, let's examine what makes an affiliate marketing program genuinely exceptional.

CHAPITRE SEVENTEEN

Case Study: The Affiliate Marketing Program of XYZ Company

Let's look at an illustration. Suppose you are the proprietor of the company XYZ. You're anxious to observe the performance of your newly launched affiliate marketing program.

A few affiliates are recruited, and they begin promoting your products. Initially, everything appeared to be going well. However, you begin to observe that sales are declining. What's happening?

It's possible that your affiliates are not targeting the appropriate audience or are not using the appropriate keywords in their ads. It is also possible that they do not provide sufficient value to their consumers.

If you want your affiliate marketing program to be successful, you must attentively monitor results and ensure that your affiliates are performing their duties correctly. Otherwise, you may be losing money rather than earning it.

We trust you found this article useful and are now prepared to launch your own successful affiliate marketing campaign.

Here are a few final considerations:
Always be willing to devote time and energy to your affiliate marketing campaigns. They will not produce themselves!

Maintain an awareness of the most recent industry developments so that you can continue to identify profitable opportunities.

Experiment with and evaluate various strategies until you discover the one that works best for you and your audience.

Have patience — triumph does not occur overnight!

And most importantly, have enjoyment; affiliate marketing should be enjoyable.

Business Models For Affiliate Marketing

Affiliate marketing is a vast field, and if you believe that it can only be used to generate passive income, you are underestimating the effectiveness of this massive online marketing strategy.

The time has come for people to take the strategy seriously and utilize the available resources to generate a steady income. The issue is that people are frequently oblivious and uninformed about the topic, preventing them from realizing its benefits. Similar considerations apply to affiliate marketing. Due to people's continued reluctance toward online income sources, the topic is still unexplored. It is still considered the greatest source of passive income, after all.

However, this chapter will alter the viewers' perspectives. Consequently, what are we awaiting? Let's delve deeply into the topic at hand.

There are numerous affiliate marketing business models that affiliates may be unaware of. Identifying the optimal affiliate business model and offer could be the first step towards achieving success. Researching the topic will provide a new perspective and a more fertile environment for growth. The disadvantage of this profession is that working on a single model for years may not yield the intended income. Therefore, altering the model may be the best option. But how can an affiliate alter the business model if they do not know it exists?

Affiliate marketing business model types

Model of Recurring Affiliate Marketing

The recurring affiliate marketing model enables affiliates to receive commissions on transactions on a recurring basis. Most affiliate programs do not offer commissions on a recurring basis. This is due to the fact that once a transaction is made through an affiliate link, the potential customer becomes a direct customer of the brand, and the role of the affiliates is eliminated after the initial sale.

However, the pattern of the recurring affiliate marketing model is distinct in that affiliates have the opportunity to earn a commission each time a consumer purchases the brand.

This business model is preferable to the "one-off" model because the latter only permits earning a one-time commission. In one-time commission business models, affiliates receive a commission only once, with no recurring earnings.

However, if a customer signs up for a monthly subscription plan through the affiliate link, the affiliate will receive a commission for the duration of the subscription for that particular customer. The commission range will vary, and the affiliate may begin with a low-priced product. In the long run, however, the affiliate will earn more money with the recurring affiliate marketing model than with the one-time affiliate marketing model. Consider joining the recurring affiliate marketing model if you are a novice in affiliate marketing and watch your monthly earnings cycle accelerate. The monthly influx of income will be an excellent motivator for you to advance.

The category of recurring affiliate business models encompasses subscription plans, membership and training programs, and software products. A few notable names mentioned below will clarify the point.

The platform provides website hosting for enterprises and website owners to online users.

Six Figure Mentors is a popular platform that offers affiliates training programs and comprehensive support. It also offers affiliates a variety of promotional products.

When business owners think of email marketing, Aweber is the first name that comes to mind.

This platform provides online business owners with the finest online support available. They can also receive SEO assistance for campaign marketing.

Organic/Natural SEO for Online Marketing

Marketing is the process of assisting customers/prospects in discovering your website/business/blog in order to grow your business, increase sales leads, or reduce customer acquisition costs. Smart marketing incorporates both SEO and PPC. It is effective search engine advertising that attracts new customers.

To be more precise, organic/natural search engine optimization is the process of optimizing a website, page, or blog to rank highly in the search engines' unpaid results. This is the most effective and least expensive method for attracting visitors, as visitors are more likely to engage on unpaid, organic results than sponsored ones.

Sixty-five percent of business websites were created with little regard for search engine optimization. That means that two-thirds of online businesses are positioned at the bottom of search engine results pages. This is a concern because 85 percent of all internet transactions are driven by search engines.

Organic optimization employs the "White Hat" technique, which includes keyword research, the positioning of key phrases in Meta tags and content, and the use of special formatting, such as headers, bold, and bullets.

Both online and offline optimization is necessary. Regularly post to directories, compose press releases, submit articles, and acquire additional backlinks to your website or blog.

Simply create a blog about your target keyword to acquire pertinent links. Link to it from your website or another blog, and maintain its accuracy and originality. 70% of search engine users visit organic sites, with 50% choosing the best results. You may attract a large number of visitors to your website or blog.

Conclusion

To commence affiliate marketing, no prior knowledge or experience is required. It has a low barrier to entry, and you can begin making money immediately. To obtain the best results, it requires dedication and focus, and you must approach it seriously.

You can join numerous affiliate networks for free and promote a variety of their affiliate offers. You can promptly begin promoting your products because some of these networks do not require permission to get started.

Although it is possible to make money without any experience in affiliate marketing, it is strongly recommended that you invest in appropriate training if you want to see significant results.

Best of success with your affiliate marketing efforts!

What You Need To Know Concerning Affiliate Commission Payment Schedules

The first compensation you receive as an affiliate is arguably the most exciting part of the process. In the end, the check or deposit notification represents all the weeks (or possibly months) of hard work, diligent promotion, and lead-hunting on your behalf. There is now evidence that your affiliate marketing efforts are beginning to produce results. Learn the fundamentals of affiliate commission payment schedules to better comprehend how the payment system for affiliate marketing programs functions.

Getting compensated

As an affiliate, you are compensated through commissions. This is a predetermined percentage of the total price of an affiliate product or service that you promoted or sold. In many cases, it can also come from a portion of the revenue generated by your team's downline members.

A schedule governs the payment of affiliate commissions. There is typically a minimum threshold and a deadline for affiliate programs, although there are exceptions.

It is easy to comprehend why affiliate programs do not instantaneously send you a check for every sale you generate. Affiliate programs must adhere to a standard when it comes to paying their affiliates to ensure a streamlined, error-free, and equitable process. A program runs the risk of becoming disjointed and inaccurate without a plan for commission payments.

Determine the commission payment schedule for your affiliate program.

Before signing up as an affiliate, it is essential to review the program's FAQ section. Frequently, the most fundamental information regarding affiliate marketing programs can be located on their website. The commission distribution schedule they've established for their affiliates should be specified in their Frequently Asked Questions section.

Contact your affiliate program or sponsor, if you have one, if the information is unavailable. When choosing an affiliate program, the frequency of affiliate commission disbursements is crucial. To avoid regrets in the future, do not join an affiliate program without this knowledge.

How frequently is the payment distributed?

The preferences of the affiliate program determine how frequently commissions are paid out. This situation is essentially beyond the authority of the affiliate. The payment schedule can vary from bimonthly to monthly. Some companies, such as LinkShare, pay out commissions weekly, which is a significantly shorter period.

What payment methods are utilized for affiliate commissions?

Typically, affiliate programs employ three techniques. These include wire transfers, cheques, and the processing of electronic payments (such as PayPal). The transaction method will determine how quickly you receive your commission payment.

If the payment is processed via electronic payment channels, it typically takes less than twenty-four hours. Checks (often sent by postal mail or courier) typically arrive within three to seven business days, but may take longer depending on the affiliate's location. Wire transfers typically take three to six business days.

Exists anything that could affect the payment schedule for affiliate commissions?

Typically, the affiliate commission distribution schedule is quite predetermined. However, there are a number of circumstances that can cause delays. The question of whether an affiliate has met the minimum earnings requirement is one of the most frequently asked.

Affiliate programs frequently require a minimal earnings threshold per pay period ranging from $10 to $100. If an employee earns less than the required minimum, his earnings will be carried over to the subsequent pay period until he reaches the required minimum. His salary will not be disclosed until then.

TECHNOLOGY

Technology facilitates life and work, provides entertainment, and facilitates the sharing of our lives and thoughts. The $500 billion software industry is also influenced by digital transformation.

As a consequence of the global economic downturn, global revenues from digital entertainment decreased to $2 trillion. However, it is anticipated to grow in the years to come, reaching $2.5 trillion by 2024.

This affiliate marketing sector is related to digital downloads, digital streaming, video games, business software, mobile technology, and other products.

Additionally, COVID-19 has had an impact on this industry. People spend more time at home imbibing digital media and working remotely via technology. Sickness and unemployment have reduced the workforce, resulting in lower physical outputs. Consequently, industries that can are utilizing digital alternatives to meet consumer demand.

PERSONAL FINANCE

This section concentrates on providing financial services to consumers, especially in competition with conventional banks. It is anticipated to increase at a compound annual growth rate of 20% over the next five years, reaching over $300 billion by 2025. Affiliate marketing in financial technology is anticipated to be worth $12 billion globally in 2019.

People want more opportunities to access, develop, and share their money. This category includes e-invoicing services, investments, cryptocurrencies, financial innovations, peer-to-peer (P2P) payments, data security, and similar services.

In regards to affiliate marketing, financial technology companies have come to their senses. Almost every industry employs this tactic to expand their market reach, with some making substantial investments in their relationships.

Registering with an Affiliate program
Joining an affiliate program is almost always free.
If credit card information is required for associate registration, you may be the victim of fraud. The majority of reputable businesses that offer affiliate programs allow consumers to sign up for free.
You will be required to provide a PayPal or bank account number, however. Remember that the corporation is acting in this manner to pay you the commission you've earned through effective sales, not to steal your money.

In certain situations, the URL of your website will be required. Simply specify the URL of the website you created earlier.

Affiliate marketing through a website.

Including affiliate links in your articles is a great way to earn money without appearing to sell. In this strategy, you will receive a commission if a user clicks on your link, is redirected to the company's website, and ultimately makes a purchase.

Make the word "purple comforters" a link to Amazon's website that only displays purple comforters, if you're writing about decor that includes purple comforters, for example. Your audience can browse Amazon's selection and potentially purchase anything they desire.

The good news is that businesses make linking to their websites relatively simple. The process for obtaining these links varies from company to company, but you can typically find a link to the product or products you're seeking relatively rapidly.

Choosing a product for promotion
Stick to marketing familiar products or services to begin with. This is known as "niche selection" among online marketers. Choose a specialization that reflects your current occupation or interests.

If you are an expert in interior design, for instance, it makes more sense to sell bedding sets than auto parts. Marketing efforts will be much more successful if you keep to selling only what you know.

Creating a target audience
You want visitors to return to your website, right? If this is the case, you must continue to offer distinct, valuable content to your audience. This is referred to by digital marketers as "content marketing."

Websites with high-quality content see repeat traffic. Thus, they may eventually click on your affiliate connections and complete a purchase.

As previously discussed, you can incorporate affiliate links into your content. The more affiliate links a website has, the more content it generates. Eventually, the law of averages will take effect, and you will begin selling.

Utilizing social media for affiliate marketing

It is a common misconception that a few random posts are sufficient for social media marketing. However, it goes much deeper than that.

Affiliate promotion is no different.

Every marketing effort requires a strategy. The process involves collecting the necessary data, identifying your advertising objectives and target audience, and customizing your advertisements for social media platforms.

Who is your intended audience, and where are they the most active and involved on social media?

Each platform takes a distinct approach to the creation and distribution of content. Thus, the demographics of consumers on each platform are distinct.

While Instagram continues to dominate, Generation Z has embraced the upstart TikTok. Twitter is where millennials gather information about current events and activities. The majority of LinkedIn users are professionals with college degrees. Everyone possesses a Facebook account.

Choosing the proper domain name
A few decades ago, it made little sense to consider potential domain names when launching a business. This is due to the fact that the website was launched after the business began operations. Operations that began online were uncommon.

It makes sense to design your company's online presence as soon as feasible in modern times. Every business must have an online presence, including a website and most likely social media. Also, for professional email addresses.

Sometimes, brands have social media identities that do not match their domain or company names. However, combining them can significantly enhance brand cohesion.

Chapter Seven- Tips
Free affiliate marketing tools
Google's Search Appliance
This is the first and predominant keyword tool. You must establish a Google Ads account to use it, which is worthwhile. Even though its value has diminished over time, the Google keyword tool is still vital. Choose a keyword for your product or service only after conducting research.

MANGOOLS Although Portent, a Google SERP clone, features a preview tool as well, I prefer Mangools'. This is an excellent alternative to the Yoast plugin, at least for your title and meta description elements, if you still need to install it on your WordPress website (oops, I shouldn't have mentioned plugins!).

Internet Marketing
This is comparable to Google Webmaster Tools in that it possesses so many powerful features that it almost exists in a different universe. It enables you to discover where your site's visitors originate and what they do once they arrive. You can even conduct website testing using Content Experiments. If you're not using Analytics, I assume you're doing something else.

How To Locate Items That Will Sell In Your Drop Shipping Store

This is the phase where many people become trapped when they first launch their Drop shipping store.

They ask themselves continuously, "What should I sell?" and "How do I know if this item will sell?"

Don't be concerned if you answered yes to one or both of these queries. I will help you!

Understand that in the "Drop shipping business," successful products are referred to as "winning products."

These are the items that your customers adore and rapidly sell out.

Once you observe sales, it is highly unlikely that you will forsake your Drop-shipping business.

Second, it is essential to recognize which products should be avoided when drop shipping.

For instance, those that may cause you future (legal) trouble or those with a high rate of return.

What are the best methods for conducting investigation for your Drop shipping business?

You now comprehend the basics of product investigation! Now let's examine how to conduct product investigation.

The first method is to perform the task manually and for no cost.

The second method is to utilize a service capable of performing the majority of product investigation tasks automatically. However, the majority of these services are costly, but there are a few that are free!

How to Conduct Free Product Research on Your Own

Examine what other prosperous Drop shippers are selling and their most popular products.

Discovering winning products is facilitated by locating successful Drop-shipping stores and examining their best-selling items.

So why would someone continue to advertise a non-profitable product?

This question can be incorporated into any of the following product research approaches!

Here, you learned how to observe each Shopify Drop shipping store's best-selling products.

The only factor that genuinely matters for this type of product research is locating additional Drop shipping stores!

Consider their newly-introduced products as a second application of this strategy.

Perhaps they will test new products, and one of them will be an untried winner!

There is always value in searching, as you never know what you might find.

1) Amazon

Amazon is the first and most apparent option!

There is a 99 percent chance that you are already familiar with Amazon lol.

Researching drop shipping products on Amazon is as simple as researching regular products.

You can learn a great deal about the types of items that are currently selling well (Best Sellers), as well as what has been trending in the last 24 hours (Movers & Shakers).

Isn't that incredible?

Movers and Shakers on Amazon

Movers & Shakers on Amazon highlights products whose sales have increased over the past 24 hours. These products are rapidly climbing the sales charts.

Not all products are appropriate for drop shipping, which is a disadvantage.

1.2) Best Sellers on Amazon

The Amazon Best Sellers store showcases the online retailer's best-selling items, as determined by sales.

Similar to the Movers and Shakers, not all products are appropriate for Drop shipping!

I suggest perusing the various categories to see if there are any products that you believe would be appealing to sell on your Drop shipping website.

Even better, if you have a specialty, you can simply select it and see what Amazon products are selling well in that area!

2) Wish

This is intended for those unfamiliar with Wish.

Wish is a prominent shopping website for Western consumers. Numerous people are familiar with Wish due to its extensive advertising efforts.

You can now benefit from this.

Simply visit Wish to view the available merchandise.

And if your Drop shipping store caters to a specific niche, you can use Wish to determine which products are popular in that area.

Look for products that have received at least 1,000 to 5,000 orders.

To rapidly locate these items, press the CTRL and F keys simultaneously, followed by the number 000.

Now, all products with at least 1,000 orders will be highlighted!

Isn't that incredible?

3) Facebook

There are numerous methods to use Facebook to research Drop shipping products!

If you follow me below, I will demonstrate each of them.

3.1) Facebook Search Box

This may be common knowledge, but I'll include it for those who are oblivious!

Simply visit Facebook and input one of the aforementioned terms in the search field.

3.2) Imitating other Drop shipping merchants

From the first method of product research, it was evident that examining other successful Drop shipping companies is a highly effective method for locating new products.

You can currently go one step further by monitoring their Facebook page.

Consequently, you will be the first to know when a new product is undergoing testing.

You can also see which varieties of Facebook advertisements performed best for them. Examine the advertised products in their most popular advertisements.

4) AliExpress

When you are ready to launch your own online Drop shipping business, you should visit the AliExpress Drop shipping Center.

This is the tool developed by AliExpress to facilitate drop shipment.

In the AliExpress Drop shipping center, you will have access to a plethora of extraordinary tools.

However, what is the best feature of the Drop shipping center?

It is entirely without cost!

5) Exchange Marketplace

Visiting Shopify's Exchange Marketplace is yet another way to find great products for your Drop shipping business.

This page contains several Shopify stores for sale, but the most important aspect is that you can select Drop shipping as your business type!

You should be aware that some Shopify Drop shipping firms for sale will be listed anonymously, while others will be accessible to the public.

Everything is visible, including the website's URL, revenue, and total number of visitors.

Now you can browse all of these Drop shipping companies that are on sale, and then visit their websites to determine which of their products are the most popular.

This will provide you with a great deal of inspiration. You have the same opportunity as they do to establish a profitable Shopify Drop shipping business and sell it for $35,000.

Remember not to duplicate anything exactly. Here, we are conducting product investigation!

6) Awesome Websites

This product research strategy is not intended for Drop shippers, but these websites will unquestionably provide you with ideas regarding what items are currently popular and which products have a high likelihood of selling well!

The first website is titled "Shut Up and Take My Money." If you haven't heard of it, "Shut Up and Take My Money" is essentially a website with an abundance of "wow"-inducing items.

These products are uncommon in conventional retail stores. Because of this, it is a great place to gather concepts for your Drop shipping business.

The second one is called Modern Touch.

This website has more expensive products, but it is a great resource for dropshipping ideas because it also offers a wide variety of dropshippable items.

In addition, they have a page titled "Sales under $25."

This will unquestionably provide you with some intriguing items that could be useful for your Drop shipping business!

7) YouTube Videos of Excellent Products

This is yet another excellent method for product investigation. Essentially, you search YouTube for videos such as:

2022 Top Ten Items Sold on AliExpress

Top Ten Amazon Items in 2022

Top 10 Wish List Items for 2022

This will result in a plethora of YouTube videos containing inventories of the most fantastic items currently available on AliExpress, Amazon, or Wish.

What is contained in each of these videos?

Indeed, these are excellent products!

Check the remarks section to see if any of the products on the list have received a great deal of positive feedback.

Using these videos for Drop shipping product research will unquestionably provide you with a great deal of inspiration.

8) Communicate with Drop shipping vendors on AliExpress

This is yet another excellent method for locating excellent Drop-shipping products!

This strategy involves locating Drop shipping suppliers on AliExpress and contacting them to inquire about products that are about to become popular, those that have recently been introduced, and those that will be available in the near future.

You must first identify the best AliExpress Drop shipping suppliers.

Preferably AliExpress sellers of these popular Drop-shipping products (or, if you're in a specific region, niche-specific suppliers).

After locating a few of these AliExpress suppliers, the next step is to contact them.

Determine what new products they intend to introduce to the market. Their newest bestsellers! You may also request an inventory of their most popular products (or both).

So that you can find items that are not yet offered by many Drop shippers.

9) CJDrop delivery

CJDrop shipping ranks second on the list of the best methods for researching Drop shipping products.

Check out their website if you're curious about what they do.

I have included them on this list due to the fact that their app contains so many products. From best-selling items to trending items and even new products.

Simply perusing the various categories will almost certainly generate new Drop-shipping product ideas!

The only requirement is that you sign up for a free account, which I believe is worthwhile given the quantity of concepts you will receive!

10) Oberlo

The amount of times a product has been imported into Drop shipping stores powered by Oberlo.

You can view the number of product imports, page views, and orders:

I would contemplate perusing multiple categories to identify a product with a high number of imports and orders. You could be at the forefront of a new product trend if you can find a product that is the exact antithesis.

If you have a specific niche, you can simply investigate it to determine what other Drop shippers are importing for their enterprises.

11) Pinterest

Pinterest is an additional excellent resource for determining what is currently fashionable and popular.

Simply search for Pinterest Pins. Consider automobiles and domestic appliances:

12) Instagram

Instagram is yet another social media platform you can use to determine what's currently trending.

This is perfect for niche Drop shipping businesses. Simply follow every Instagram page that falls into that category.

Thus, you will receive a notification whenever a tribute is posted on one of the pages you follow.

If you find an Instagram page with a live shoutout, you can decide for yourself whether the product is worth selling (read the remarks!).

The best part is that you can now simply browse through your feed once or twice per day (on the Instagram account where you follow all these accounts) to check for new shoutout-containing posts. Also, remember to check your Instagram Stories.

Division 4

How do I create a successful affiliate marketing and dropshipping strategy?

Marketing your dropshipping business is essential unless you only use third-party marketplaces, which is not recommended for those who wish to generate extremely high profits through dropshipping. How do you reach the intended market of your niche? Moreover, even if you have a steady source of income to cover the expense, how can you manage this situation without immediately exceeding your budget and maximize your investment? Paid advertising has many benefits, but having a platform in your numerous online interactions is the most effective form of advertising.

Optimization for search engine performance

We've talked extensively about SEO, particularly keyword research, and we cannot emphasize enough how essential it is to work with Google. My final recommendation is to hire an SEO expert to audit your website and provide you with a plan for enhancing SEO after you have already published content.

Google considers a variety of factors when determining your website's position in the search results.

- Develop content. In order for Google to index your website, it must contain content. In addition to requiring content for your website, you also need original, non-copied content that has not been taken from other websites on the internet. The more content you have, the more Google can index it, and the more original your content is, the less likely you are to be penalized for plagiarism.
- Keywords. Google searches for keywords and key phrases for apparent reasons, but how you handle them may matter much more than you think. It is essential to avoid using terms in an

unnatural or excessive manner. Use a keyword no more than once every 100–300 words, especially if doing so would seem inappropriate.

• Images and motion pictures. Google's image and video queries will function with your photographs and videos if you've utilized them properly. This may make it easier for people to discover your website and boost its position in search engine results.

• Backlinks. A backlink is any link linking to another website. The more effective these sites are at linking to your website and assisting you climb Google's page rankings, the greater their value to you. Backlinks are a baffling concept, and people frequently post links to any website they can discover. This strategy may sometimes be detrimental to your website, as low-cost providers frequently rely on obsolete SEO techniques and position links to your website on irrelevant websites. It is essential to obtain only natural hyperlinks, or at the very least, to work with an SEO professional.

Technical details are essential. Amazingly, Shopify houses all of its technological components in a single location. If your online store is not powered by Shopify, you should hire an SEO expert with web design expertise to assist you in identifying any areas of your website that need to be modified due to poor coding in order to enhance both user experience and search engine optimization.

The most important takeaway from this is that you need original, high-quality content that includes photographs and videos (if possible) and is highly compatible with a variety of web browsers and operating systems. SEO requires much more than simply understanding and applying these terms.

SEO is a natural method to increase traffic, although it is a longer-term strategy than paid advertising.

On social media

It would be absurd for a specialized business proprietor to completely disregard social networking in the present day. Idealistically, you should be able to integrate into the online community of your potential consumers, either by actively participating there or by creating a space just for them. Creating a Facebook group for them may be the best option, especially if you're adept at interacting with people online.

This not only provides you insight into your target market and feedback about your company, but if applicable, it also establishes you as a caring community member. This may require a great deal of work, but the secret to making it completely autonomous is to take your time. As with other platforms, you can always hire a contractor for assistance with this.

Always keep in mind that content reigns supreme. You cannot simply irritate people with spam and impolite comments and then expect too much in return. Before you can market your business, you must first contribute to the creation of value.

Message List

It has long been considered one of the most effective strategies for attracting and retaining an online audience. Possessing a mailing list makes it simpler to communicate with clients who were willing to sign up for one. You can promote your email list on your blog, your store's website, and on social media. Providing them with something of value is the simplest way to convince them to join your mailing list. This could be a discount code, a complimentary eBook, special offers and content, etc.

Using paid services such as ConstantContact or MailChimp to manage your mailing list is much more effective than attempting to copy and paste multiple email addresses into your Gmail account.

Product Assessments

Product evaluations can affect the success or failure of sales. Allowing these on your online store and ensuring that you carry only high-quality products are crucial steps for enticing customers to promote your products for you. Remember that purchasing fake reviews is not a good notion.

Avoid spam

The absolute prohibition against employing deceptive marketing strategies and the fact that spam rarely generates sales are two of the most essential points to remember. It will not generate significant revenue to respond to every Facebook post. Additionally, posting on forums to promote a store is rarely effective. If you want to use these channels for marketing, you must be intimately connected and involved with members of your target audience.

Even though there is much more to marketing than these broad overviews, they will assist you in developing a marketing strategy that suits your objectives, budget, and target audience. I do not recommend relying solely on paid advertisements or on search engine optimization. Marketing and consumer engagement should be approached with an all-encompassing approach.

Mistakes and pitfalls to avoid
Particularly if you choose a poor product to advertise, you shouldn't be too hard on yourself. In fact, you may occasionally find yourself returning to the drafting board.

We will err when conducting business, and that is acceptable. Our blunders will serve as our teachers, and they will be extremely severe and dreadful ones. They will ultimately contribute to our growth.

Now, one fast fix is to learn from the errors made by other marketers in order to avoid making costly mistakes. In addition to pointing you in the right direction, pioneers are there to help you avoid potential dangers.

The following are several of my most significant mistakes that you should avoid:

Selecting an extremely competitive product

Now, I should point out that this is a fairly common novice mistake. In my opinion, every dropshipper will commit an error at some point.

How did I acquire that? There was a time when I thought Bluetooth speakers were a terrific product.

It seemed ideal for online distribution, in my opinion. I possess extensive knowledge about them as well. I once owned a number of these speakers.

I examined the competition and found that numerous individuals sell these on eBay and Amazon.

I browse for search terms and determine the product's popularity. In recent months, tens of thousands of queries have been conducted for Bluetooth speakers, and the patterns indicate a consistent and rising demand for the product.

Additionally, it is a popular search term on social media. I observed that individuals were advertising these items on Facebook Marketplace at the time, and that many people had concerns.

I believed the product would be successful and that I could share in its financial success. Yes, many other retailers are currently profiting from it, and they have unquestionably already captured a portion of the market share.

I estimate that there are several hundred individuals searching elsewhere. I believed I could establish myself there.

Was it a prudent choice? Not at all, no.

Since then, I've realized that endeavoring to enter a crowded market is a mistake waiting to occur. Yes, there is a possibility that I could capture a portion of the market.

However, I did not anticipate the price competition among competitors. They were experienced, whereas I was just beginning. They can continue to operate even with minimal profits, but I required the funds to finance the expansion of my business.

To make a lengthy story short, I eventually yielded to the pressure.

• Differentiating forgeries

I repeat that not all Chinese-made items are imitations. It is not required that the product be manufactured in China or another tranquil nation. Anywhere in the world can produce imitations.

Ultimately, producers of counterfeits and imitations will be identified. They have not yet been captured by the FBI (or another agency responsible for capturing them).

Don't misjudge me. Counterfeits are available for purchase on the open market. This material is acquired. There is absolutely no doubt in my mind.

However, here is some advice based on my experience: avoid imitations. Although this did not occur to me, I learned from a colleague that selling these items online could land you in legal trouble.

In light of this, you should thoroughly investigate your suppliers, especially if they are new or claim to be able to provide the same products for significantly less money.

If their offer seems too good to be true, you can bet your last dollar that it is genuine. It is possible that they are selling counterfeit products. Oh, they can easily establish a new provider website and flee. Legally, the odds are piled against you if you have just started a new sole proprietorship as a novice.

Important advice: Never do it.

Marketing a designer product

The category of designer products encompasses all recognizable brands on the market. Due to their consistent demand, they may also be quite enticing to sell.

They are also extremely expensive, which may cause you to consider increasing your markup. Do not attempt to sell them is an additional piece of crucial advice.

Likewise, this is based on experience. Do you think selling designer products will increase your profit margin? It is a fact that the profit margins for these items are quite minimal.

Large brands and retailers can accept a low return on investment because they can tolerate it. They can retain their enormous wealth. Neither the dropshipper nor yourself.

Your purchasing power is initially at jeopardy. Suppose there are returns, then what? Large box stores are able to do this because, candidly, they have more capital than our smaller businesses. Until you have that, you shouldn't experiment with these items, especially if you're just beginning out.

• Top Dropshipping Products Thanks to me, you no longer have to seek for some of the hottest items on the market.

Be aware that you can evaluate the dropshipping viability of these products using Google Trends and Keyword Planner.

What items are on the list?

Where Can I Locate Reliable Dropship Suppliers?

Some merchants are outstanding or respectable, while others are subpar or even awful. All new dropshipping businesses must deal with this reality; consequently, you must be aware of the characteristics to look for in suppliers, how to interact with suppliers, and the hazards to avoid.

Before contacting vendors, comply with the law.

Before you begin searching for and contacting potential suppliers and wholesalers, you must have legally established and properly documented your business. Before suppliers will contemplate conducting business with you, they will require verification of your legitimacy. Since suppliers are accustomed to businesspeople seeking information, they will respond to your basic inquiries without requiring proof of your legitimacy.

Suppliers and wholesalers will not work with unauthorized businesses; therefore, you must be properly established and adhere to all state regulations in order to obtain permission. However, wholesalers have learned the hard way that too many individuals attempt to defraud them. Consequently, ensure that all of your documentation is in order and initiate the development of solid relationships with your suppliers.

Effective online vendor inquiry

Finding the suppliers and wholesalers you want to work with will require some ingenuity because they are notoriously eccentric and fiercely autonomous. Instead of attempting to evade business proprietors, suppliers simply pursue their own objectives. To obtain the best results, you must conduct exhaustive searches and adhere to the suggestions provided.

Deeper Searches

Suppliers do not place a high value on advertising their products. To obtain the information you require, you will need to examine several search results with attention. Frequently, when searching for a particular product, the official website of the provider does not appear until Page 6 or Page 10 of the search results. If you persevere, you will be rewarded.

Modify your search's parameters

It is insufficient to simply search for Vendor X or Item Y; you must modify your queries. Your search results will be acceptable at best. Create a list of synonyms for terms such as supplier and wholesaler, and then conduct separate queries on each synonym. To achieve the best search results, use a variety of language and search terms.

Functional yet unappealing

Typically, when you visit a website, you look for things that appeal to you, things that grab your attention rapidly, and websites that hold your attention with engaging web copy and high-quality images.

Especially new businesses may find wholesalers' and suppliers' websites to be aesthetically dated and antiquated. They do not waste valuable time and resources on developing websites to attract prospective customers because they are aware that consumers will seek them out. Learn to look beyond the external design of their websites; it does not always indicate a poor source or inferior products.

The usefulness of purchased vendor directories

The use of supplier directories is a fiercely debated topic, as some consider it an unnecessary luxury once suppliers have been selected. There is no precise response; each entrepreneur must make their own choice.

These databases are quite useful to have on hand because they are organized and categorized so that you can locate all the suppliers for a particular item in one place, and they are frequently updated. Before adding businesses to their paid supplier directories, the majority of the prominent providers of paid supplier directories conduct background checks to ensure that all of their listings are genuine suppliers and wholesalers.

Having access to a large number of alternative suppliers for your specialty items is a further advantage of using paid directories.

Supplier directories are a useful and convenient tool to have when you need them or want to begin expanding your business, but they are not a necessity.

Other Strategies

Consider selecting an alternative from a more specialized niche. Imagine that you come across a specialized eBook, such as one that explains how to become a successful flower arranger. Even though the audience is smaller and the product appears less exciting, your product is now distinct.

Additionally, you can rapidly connect with flower arrangers by commenting on a few flower blogs. In addition, it will be much easier for you to drive your sales page to the top of Google's search results for "flower arranging eBook." In addition, it has a unique USP that makes it easy to sell.

However, it is even better to consider your current marketing channels. What connections are available to you? Where can one travel great distances?

Buying a product that will appeal to your audience makes sense if your website is already renowned and has a large following.

Several Products

Also, remember that you have the option of offering a variety of products. Another important advantage of selling digital products is the ability to quickly add or remove items from your website without spending hours writing and preparing content.

Multiple product sales have advantages and disadvantages. If you have a large website and employ soft-sale strategies, it is excellent to sell multiple products (see the next chapter). This allows you to offer varying prices to numerous customer types. However, focusing on a single product at a time will enable you to streamline your website so that customers are directed to a single page — the purchasing page — and generate more buzz and excitement around that product.

Add Affiliate Links To Your Free Reports

One of the reasons you would write announcements for free is to distribute affiliate links. Here is some background information on how to incorporate a link into the text of your free reports and generate substantial income from your efforts.

One of the most important things you must do is ensure that the placement of links within the text of the free report is understandable. The objective is for the reader to discover the link while perusing the body of the report.

The existence of the link will be obvious, as it will typically appear in blue, underlined text. You want the reader to encounter the link, determine that it is relevant to what he or she is reading, and decide to select it before continuing.

This is less likely to occur if the names of your links fail to capture the reader's attention. Using link names that jar the reader away from the content without a clear purpose increases the likelihood that he or she will not only click on the link, but also cease reading and move on to another web page.

In terms of the logistics of inserting a hyperlink into your report, the following are the essential steps:

First, you will need to create a rudimentary article with already-established links. Open a draft article in your word processor to accomplish this. Additionally, have the website that you want the link to lead the reader to open in a browser.

Select the URL you wish to convert into a link, then right-click on the cursor or press "Control" and "C" on your keyboard to copy the URL. Copy the hyperlink and paste it into your blank word processing document. Cut and paste all the URLs you intend to use for your free announcement to advance the process.

In effect, you are establishing a source page that you will be able to utilize in the subsequent step, which involves injecting links into the text of your free report.

Step two of your assignment is to compose your announcement. Include the keywords that you intend to use as link names in the text. This will provide you with the easiest method for inserting the connections, as the locations will already be marked.

Remember that you want the text to progress smoothly and hold the reader's attention. The links should appear as if they are a natural part of the announcement, rather than as if they were tacked on for no apparent purpose.

Pay close attention to how you construct the report, and you should be able to include a large number of links and valuable keywords that will help your free report appear in search results.

Next, start inserting your connections. You can accomplish this by perusing your entire report. When you reach a suitable location for the insertion of one of the links, switch to your saved source document and locate the link you wish to insert.

Utilize the same methods to copy and paste the link as you did when creating the resource page. This link will be highlighted in blue or underscored in the body of your test, depending on which criteria you have assigned.

Note that if you are using Microsoft Word to produce your free report, you can simply highlight the text you want to link to and then click the "Insert Hyperlink" toolbar tab.

You will then be presented with a screen that allows you to paste or type the URL you desire to associate with the assigned word or phrase. This will automatically generate the link in your document and allow you to use any keyword or keyphrase to link to an affiliate ad or website.

Ensure you save your document after inserting connections. It is now merely a consequence of converting the document to PDF format. You can do this with Word or you can download the word processing program from http://www.openoffice.com.

Simply copy and paste your announcement and then select the "PDF" icon to create a PDF. After that, all you need to do is locate the appropriate home for your free report and start promoting it. From there, you will quickly realize some income from your actions.

Submission of Your Free Report for Publication

The next item on your to-do list will be to locate a home on the Internet for your free announcement, which you have already written and to which you have added links to several affiliate products.

You will also need to enhance your strategies for distributing the free report in order to generate interest in both the report and the affiliate links it contains. Here are some tips to help you establish a permanent online presence for your free report and distribute it in favorable locations.

Creating a website is a potential means of finding a location for your free report. Today, it is very easy to find affordable domain name and hosting packages that cost less than one dollar per month to administer.

The benefit of having the complimentary report hosted on a remote server and displayed on your website is that you can update the report at any time.

In addition, you have control over which affiliates can post advertisements on your free announcement pages, and you can update the links whenever you like. This greatly simplifies the creation of free reports, as multiple free reports can be posted on multiple pages under one domain name.

Once you've established a permanent online location for your free announcement, you can begin the process of enhancing it. One of the best locations to start is on websites that permit classified advertisements.

Write a brief summary, no longer than one paragraph, that describes your free announcement to the reader. Include something that will serve as a prelude and pique the reader's interest. Include the URL to your free advertisement. Utilize classified ad websites with high search engine rankings. In just a few days, this should generate some traffic to your free announcement.

Another alternative is to have your free announcement listed in Ebook directories. Look for catalogs that feature expression-related topics pertinent to the subject of your free report. This will make it easier for people searching online for evidence to discover the link to your free announcement. This strategy is a bit less direct than classified advertisements, but it can still generate tremendous traffic for your free announcement.

Targeting websites that invite authors to write articles on a variety of topics is an additional method for promoting your free report.

Create a two- to five-hundred-word essay on a subject that relates to some aspect of the evidence discovered in your free announcement. Incorporate a link to the free report either in the article's body or the author's description. Choose one of the article sites that has a high probability of ranking well with search engines, and you may see a substantial influx of traffic as a result.

Using your complimentary announcement to generate sales requires three fundamental components. You must first have a free announcement that is engaging and informative. If the reader is not engaged by the announcement, there is a good chance he or she will never observe the links. Maintain their interest long enough and effectively enough to convince them to explore the links.

Second, ensure that the evidence is pertinent to the interconnections. No one would want to link from a free announcement about a tinned food drive to a website that sells grain. The jump must be rational.

Ensure that you include as many links as possible without overcrowding the report. The greater the number of links included, the greater the likelihood that a reader will click through, see something he or she enjoys, and agree to purchase a product or stocks. Keeping these ideas in mind, you will discover that creating free announcements is well worth your time.

Maintaining Affiliates' Interest And Participation

Managing affiliate programs has never been easier than it is now, thanks to the available tools and support. In contrast, it is essential to get affiliates enthusiastic and increase sales. as easy as that. If your company's future success depends on the performance of your affiliates, give them everything they need to be successful. Completed successfully. It's possible that you're reading this because you have an affiliate program in place for your products. If this is the case, you should be aware that many of those who join your affiliate program do not end up having recurrent contact with the individual or individuals. However, you can reduce the number of non-contributors by contacting them and reminding them of their registration information and the URL of the website where they can view their contributions. Imagination is necessary. Don't neglect to keep them informed of any changes to product lines or operational procedures. One of the most essential aspects of maintaining motivation is to avoid maintaining contact with others. Remember that your top priority should be merchants, and communicate with them frequently or frequently. It is essential to keep track of your worst producers and to maintain regular contact with them, as well as to maintain continuous business with them. The lack of leadership among them is the primary reason why the majority of coworkers do not follow instructions, advice, etc. Changes can be made by simply putting them in writing. Marketing training that you could potentially sell to non-affiliates is recommended but not required.

It is free for your affiliates. Avoid allowing your marketing materials and ideas to become obsolete. You should also provide your stakeholders with fresh content. Utilization on a regular basis; to use frequently. Providing them with simple textual references and a single graphic advertisement generates a significant amount of interest. Create promotional materials, such as sales letters, reviews, advertisements, banners of different sizes, and anything else that comes to mind. Ensure your affiliates are aware of the content's availability. Never neglect to seek advice from those who have already provided insightful feedback on your writing. Additionally, you can conduct meetings online. Establish call spaces in which your stakeholders can conduct virtual meetings. regular monthly get-togethers Remember to respond to any doubts, listen to motivational speeches, and discuss anything else you can think of to motivate the meetings. If you want to succeed, you must give credit where credit is due to your affiliates. Likewise, it is essential to emphasize its significance. Your regular monthly contribution supports the newsletter of your affiliate's best performers. Award token quantities to contributors for whom, if successful, you may establish a payment schedule. A framework that incentivizes increased commissions and sales volume. Always exert your utmost effort for

Your software will assist your affiliates in achieving financial success. And if they are profitable, you are as well. In addition to success, monetary benefit is also a consequence. In other terms, if they are successful, you are successful.

What Is The Level Of Competition In Affiliate Marketing?

When watching a football game on television, it is evident that the conflict at the line of scrimmage determines whether a team wins or loses. The objectives of offensive plays are to obtain yards while also protecting the quarterback.

The objective of defensive plays is to sack the quarterback or close any holes that would enable the offense to gain yards. Coaches and quarterbacks receive credit for victories and responsibility for losses, but the outcome of the war is determined in the trenches.

Affiliate marketing is similar to a football game, but without the bumps and muscle soreness. Affiliate marketers must create both offensive and defensive maneuvers to be successful in the affiliate marketing arena.

If you are one of several marketers offering the same products to the same consumers, you must have a strategy to capture at least your fair share of the market and preferably more.

There is intense competition in every niche market on the Internet. If it is not competitive, there will not be a large consumer base to sell to. Online marketing operates in this manner across all segments.

Perhaps you have an extensive and impressive inventory of paying customers. I adore it! It indicates that you have won multiple affiliate marketing competitions previously. There are continually new marketers seeking to add your clients to their mailing lists.

Many of the names and email addresses on your list and your competitors' lists are likely to be identical. Possessing a roster is not sufficient to ensure success when selling affiliate products. You must devise offensive strategies to ensure that consumers choose you over your competitors when making purchases.

So, you inquire, what can I do to ensure that my customers will make purchases? One word describes the answer: singular!

You must be distinctive. You must offer something that entirely separates you from your competitors. To have your offer accepted, you must make it more alluring to purchase a product or service from you than from one of your competitors.

If you just sent out an email promoting a product or service for which you are an affiliate marketer, you should be aware that dozens, if not hundreds, of other marketers are doing the same thing, and many of them are sending emails to the same clients as you. You must take steps to ensure that your customers buy from you; you must stand out.

There are numerous ways to distinguish oneself. One strategy is to have demonstrated expertise in the industry in which the product or service is offered. You must have both credibility and visibility established. To establish credibility and visibility requires effort. It requires a great deal of time, effort, and labor.

By producing and promoting articles and E-books, participating in blogs and forums, appearing as an expert on teleconferences and webinars, etc., one can increase their visibility and credibility. The reality is that consumers purchase from you when they know and trust you. Even if your competitors offer a superior deal or more incentives, customers will still purchase from you.

Individuals detest purchasing from strangers. For many customers, the Internet is a vast, impersonal, and occasionally frightening universe. They desire to conduct business with someone they know and can depend on. The greatest investment of time, effort, and energy you will ever make is time, effort, and energy spent on establishing your credibility and visibility. In the Internet marketing industry, reputation is paramount.

Your credibility differentiates you.

Providing your customers with a compelling reason to purchase from you is another crucial step you can take to ensure they do business with you instead of a competitor and use a product or service for which you are an affiliate marketer. Offer an incentive or multiple bonuses that increase the perceived value of the product you are marketing.

Regardless of the niche or product being advertised, you may discover free bonuses that will increase the value of the product if it is purchased from you.

If you are promoting an E-Book about Internet marketing, for instance, you may include several additional free E-Books that cover various aspects of the topic.

Both PLR websites and E-Book banks and repositories provide the option to obtain eBooks. People appear to have an insatiable appetite for complimentary utilities. There are many on the Internet, and you can be certain that some of them will complement the product or service you are attempting to market.

You will improve the product without charge, whereas other marketers selling the same product as you will simply send marketing emails recommending the product to their lists.

Add more! Include giveaways! Assistance with the use of the purchased product or service is preferable to enhancements and bonuses. You can offer a complimentary teleseminar that improves or simplifies the use of your product or service to individuals who purchase it.

If you plan far enough in advance, you may even be able to invite the product or service's creator to speak at your event. People enjoy teleseminars and appreciate complimentary items. When the two are combined, you have a winning play that could result in a touchdown.

People will purchase the necessary products and services if they have a need for them. You will not need to give away your profit if you work harder and construct incentive bonuses that encourage consumers to purchase the products and services they need from you.

Give neither a discount nor a rebate on the product. Instead, increase the price of the product. Keep in mind that adding value to the product or service you're endeavoring to sell is preferable to devaluing it. A discount or refund might not always be perceived as valuable. They sometimes perceive it as an attempt to convince them to purchase a product that was originally not worth the full price.

Budget-conscious customers will only utilize a refund or discount. The dependable customers will compare offers to select the best incentives. Providing the best bonus incentives will attract the best customers, allowing you to always charge the maximum price for any advertised product or service.

Configuring and Optimizing Your Ads

Now that you have selected a web host, a domain name, and a design for your website, you can move on to the enjoyable part.You should have already selected the type of products you wish to promote in order to earn money and located a suitable affiliate program (Amazon Associates is a good starting point, but there are many others).

Once you've joined your preferred affiliate program and been granted permission to promote their products or services, it's time to get down to business.

You can use advertisements that have already been designed and approved by most affiliate programs on your affiliate website.These are typically straightforward to incorporate directly into your website using HTML code, which you can copy and paste into your website's code.Many programs will provide a variety of advertisements, including banner ads of various formats, pop-up ads, text ads, etc.Which ones you choose will depend on the design of your website and how you intend to market your product.

However, simply placing an advertisement on your website is insufficient for effective

Customers prefer to learn as much as possible about the company or brand as well as the product or service they are considering purchasing prior to making a purchase.Therefore, it is essential to write product descriptions for the merchandise you're promoting.A good affiliate marketing website will have a distinct page for each product it promotes, each with a compelling and engaging description that inspires purchase.The more data, the better!

Optimization for Search Engines If you want your new business to be successful, optimizing your affiliate site for search engine crawlers is very essential.For example, if you are promoting women's apparel, you want your website to rank as highly as possible in Google's search results when a user types "women's apparel" into the search bar and selects "Go."Optimization of search engines ought to be a top priority as a consequence of this.

When it comes to search engine optimization, there are a number of different things you need to do, and you should do them both on and off your website.If you've never done SEO before and don't know much about it, it might be a good idea to talk to a digital marketing company or an SEO expert to get some help.

Off-Page SEO Google ranks websites based on a variety of factors, but what happens on your page isn't the only thing that matters.Google values links to your page highly if they are genuine, authentic, and originate from a reputable source.A local newspaper, a popular blog, or even a popular social media profile could serve as link sources.

A greater number of authentic links to your page can result in a higher page rank.

Using guest posts is one of the most effective ways to acquire links.In the past, link-building had a poor reputation because website owners abused it by spamming forums or placing links back to their page in irrelevant places in order to acquire more links.You will not, however, behave in this way.A link that is posted in a "black hat" manner could result in a penalty from Google. One quality link is more valuable than a hundred subpar links.Instead, seek out credible, pertinent blogs that will allow you to contribute as a guest author.You will be able to create a guest post that is germane to your website and allows you to naturally include the link.

In addition to guest posting, there are numerous other methods for generating authentic, trustworthy links to your website in order to boost SEO.These include doing something newsworthy to appear in an article on a local news organization's website, including links to your website in business listings, and requesting that relevant bloggers assess your website.

On-Page SEO While what you do off of your page is essential for SEO, your website and pages play a significant role in search engine optimization and how high you rank in Google Search Results.Your website's content is a crucial element.Include the types of keywords your site's visitors will use to find you when composing product descriptions and other content.Nonetheless, it is vital to ensure that these keywords appear naturally.If this is not possible, it is essential to create keyword-based content.

Adding new content to your website is also a good method to improve SEO.For instance, you could carry out this in the form of a business blog, which you could use to write articles that provide responses to frequently requested questions, investigate various methods of utilizing the products that you sell, or even provide reviews of your own products.Keep in mind that the images you use on your website can also appear in Image Search results; therefore, textual content is not the only factor that matters for SEO.

Your website's user-friendliness is also very essential to search engine optimization.In addition to having informative content, your website should be easy to navigate and not confuse visitors.Your objective is to keep visitors on your page for as long as possible so that you can provide them with additional product information and encourage them to make a purchase.

In addition to other factors, it is also important to consider how quickly a page loads.Your site's and pages' load times can have a significant effect on SEO, as Google favors sites that load quickly and easily.In addition, consumers may become irritated by a slow-loading website, resulting in a loss of business.

Lastly, creating your website mobile-friendly is an absolute requirement.This is essential for both your reputation and SEO, as Google's most recent major algorithm updates favor mobile-friendly websites over non-responsive ones.It is imperative that your website has a responsive design that looks and functions well on all devices, as a growing number of customers use mobile devices to search for and buy products and services online.

Let me suggest a website where you can purchase a domain and web hosting at a very reasonable price, because I love you so much: Bluehost.

Optimizing Your Ads

Now that you've chosen a domain name, a web host, and a design for your website, it's time to have some fun! You should have already selected the categories of products you will promote to earn money, as well as a suitable affiliate network (Amazon Associates is a good starting point, but there are many others). After registering with your preferred affiliate network and receiving permission to advertise on their behalf, it is time to get to work.

On your affiliate website, you can utilize the pre-designed and pre-approved advertisements provided by the majority of affiliate networks. These are typically straightforward to add immediately to your website using HTML code, which you simply copy and paste into your website's code. Numerous systems provide a variety of ad formats, including pop-up ads, text ads, and banner ads of various sizes, among others. Which ones you choose will depend on the layout of your website and the advertising strategy you employ.

However, simply placing an advertisement on your website is insufficient to promote it effectively. Customers desire as much information as possible prior to making a purchase, not only about the product or service they are considering but also about the company or brand. Therefore, it is essential to provide product descriptions for the products that you advertise. Each product promoted on a website with effective affiliate marketing will have its own page with an engaging and persuasive description that encourages the consumer to make a purchase. The superior, the more instructive!

Search Engine Marketing

To ensure the success of your new venture, it is essential to optimize your affiliate website for search engine spiders. When a user types "women's clothing" into Google's search bar and selects "Go," you'd want your website to rank as highly as possible in the search results. Therefore, search engine optimization should be given high priority.

To optimize your website for search engines, you must engage in a variety of on- and off-site activities. If you have never performed SEO before and have limited knowledge of the subject, it may be a good idea to contact an SEO expert or digital marketing firm for assistance.

Off Page SEO

Google employs a variety of metrics to determine how to rank websites, so your page's activity is not the only factor. As long as they are authentic, legitimate, and originating from a reputable source, backlinks to your website are extremely valuable to Google. Link sources include a prominent blog, a well-known social media page or profile, a local news organization, and even a local news outlet. Your page's ability to achieve a higher ranking depends on the number of authentic links pointing back to it.

Guest posting is one of the most effective link-building strategies. In the past, link-building had a negative reputation due to the fact that some website proprietors abused it by spamming forums or randomly inserting links to their page in unrelated locations. However, you are not going to do this. Google may penalize you if you employ "black hat" link-building strategies. Instead, search for credible, pertinent blogs that will accept your guest post. Thus, you can create a guest post that is pertinent to your website and allows you to incorporate the link naturally.

In addition to guest posting, there are a number of other methods for generating authentic, reliable links back to your website in order to improve SEO. These include taking steps to be featured in a notable article on the website of a regional news outlet, including links to your website in business listings, and soliciting reviews from relevant bloggers.

On Page SEO

It is essential to remember that your website and pages themselves play a significant role in search engine optimization and how highly you rank in the Google Search Results, despite the fact that what you do off-page is essential for SEO. The website's content is one of its most vital components. When producing product descriptions and other website content, it is prudent to employ the types of keywords that your consumers will employ. Nonetheless, it is essential that these keywords appear organically. Creating content based on these terms is essential if this cannot be accomplished.

In addition, adding new content to your website is an excellent SEO technique. This could take the form of a company blog in which you address frequently asked questions, investigate various applications for the products you sell, and even evaluate your own products. Remember that SEO isn't just about the text on your website; it's also about the images you use, which may appear in Image Search results.

Additionally, website usability is essential for search engine optimization.

In addition to having beneficial content, your website should be easy to navigate and not lead visitors astray. Your objective is to keep visitors on your page for as long as feasible so that they can learn more about your products and be persuaded to make a purchase.

The quantity of time required for a page to load is another factor that must be considered. Google favors websites that load quickly and without issue; therefore, the time it takes for your website and its pages to load can have a direct impact on your SEO. In addition, users may find a slow-loading website annoying, which could cost you business.

Last but not least, it is essential that your website is mobile-friendly. Due to Google's recent significant algorithm updates, which favor mobile-friendly websites over those that are not, this is essential for your reputation and SEO. Given the increasing number of customers who use their mobile devices to search for and purchase products and services online, it is imperative that your website has a responsive design that appears and functions well on any device.

Some Requirements For Every Marketer

Every affiliate marketer searches continuously for the most lucrative industry with the highest payout. Sometimes they believe there is a straightforward formula for it. The circumstance is more complex than that. It's just clever marketing strategies that have withstood the test of time after years of effort and dedication.

Some strategies have been successful in the past with online marketing and are still effective now with online affiliate marketing. You can increase your sales and succeed in online affiliate marketing by implementing these three marketing strategies.

What do these three tactics accomplish?

1. Developing unique web pages to promote each of your products

Not everything can be combined to reduce hosting costs. It is preferable to have a website that only sells products.

Include product evaluations whenever possible so that site visitors can gain an understanding of the product's capabilities. Include customer reviews from individuals who have used the product. Check to see if these clients are willing to have their names and images displayed on the website for the product you are marketing.

As a supplementary page on the website, you can also compose articles demonstrating the product's application. Ensure that the pages are engaging and interesting, and include calls to action. Each headline should persuade the reader to click through, read further, or contact you. Emphasize your unique selling characteristics. This will make it simpler for your audience to comprehend the page's topic and encourage them to continue reading.

2. Provide your readers with complimentary reports.

If at all possible, position them at the very top of your website, where they cannot be missed. Try to compose autoresponder letters that will be sent to individuals who submit their personal information on your sign-up form. According to studies, a transaction is frequently concluded on the eighth contact with a prospect.

With a single web page, only one of two outcomes is possible: a closed transaction or a prospect exiting the site and never returning. By sending them helpful information at a predetermined time, you can inform them that the sale has ended and remind them of the products they thought they wanted. Ensure that the text emphasizes specific reasons for purchasing the product. Avoid sounding like an advertisement.

Concentrate on essential details, such as how your product can make life easier and more enjoyable. Use enticing subject lines in email. As much as possible, avoid using the term "free" because some antiquated spam filters still toss this type of information into the trash before anyone reads it.

Convince those who have downloaded your free reports that they are missing out if they do not purchase your products or services.

Attract visitors who are specifically interested in your products.

Consider how many visitors will abandon your website and never return if they are uninterested in your offerings.

Develop material for e-zines and e-reports. This method allows you to locate publications that are geared toward your target audience, and what you have posted may capture their interest.

Attempt to produce at least two 300-to-600-word articles per week. By continuously composing and updating these articles, you can attract up to 100 targeted visitors per day to your website.

Never neglect that only 1 in 100 people will probably purchase your goods or use your services. According to the average estimate, if you can drive 1,000 targeted visitors to your website in a single day, you may expect to make 10 sales.

If you give the aforementioned strategies some thought, they do not appear to be particularly difficult to implement. It only requires a little time from you and a strategy.

Utilize these suggestions for various affiliate marketing campaigns. You can maintain a reliable source of income while prospering in this industry, unlike other marketers.

Consider also the substantial salaries you will earn!

www.ingramcontent.com/pod-product-compliance
Lightning Source LLC
Chambersburg PA
CBHW050248120526
44590CB00016B/2269